D1294773

COUNTRY CHIC KITCHENS

A Precious Guide to Italian Style and Cooking

LOFT

COUNTRY CHIC KITCHENS. A PRECIOUS GUIDE TO ITALIAN STYLE AND COOKING

Editorial coordinator:
Simone K. Schleifer

Assistant to editorial coordination:
Aitana Lleonart

Editor:
Daniela Santos Quartino

Recipes:
Lucia Lazari

Art director:
Mireia Casanovas Soley

Design and layout coordination:
Claudia Martínez Alonso

Layout:
Cristina Simó

Translation:
Cillero & de Motta

Copyright photos:
Congedo Editore

Photographers:
Wendy Arm, Walter & Laura Leonardi

Editorial project:
2009 © Congedo Editore / LOFT Publications

ISBN: 978-84-92463-91-6

Printed in Spain

SPECIAL THANKS TO:
Lele and Elena Amoroso, Leo Ancona, Betti Bentivoglio, Simona Bentivoglio, Serena Buttiglione, Carlo Capasa, Donatella Caprioglio, Stefania Nardi Caputo, Roberta Castriota Scanderbeg, Adele Cezzi, Mariella De Benedetto, Maricla Fedele, Marina Forni, Antonella Galasso, Marco Ippolito, Enea Mariotti, Elisabetta Massaro, Paola Montagna, Maria Antonietta Petruzzi, Anna Pio, Marilena Poddi, Giovanna Sangiovanni, Enza Santese, Maria Scupola, Fabrizia Seracca Guerrieri, Maria Lucia Seracca Guerrieri, Giuliana Sguera, Mercedes Turgi Prosperi de Serconforti, Joan Welford, Gianni Zizzi.

INDEX

INTRODUCTION   5

SPRING   6
   The Grace of Time   8
   Country Aristocrat   16
   Nature Inside   20
   An Architect's Refuge   26
   Setting the Stage   30
   Spring Recipes   36

SUMMER   56
   In Black and White   58
   The Perfect Balance   64
   Turquoise Delight   70
   Aquamarine Humor   76
   Sophisticated Nature   84
   Summer Recipes   90

AUTUMN   110
   The Elegance of Simplicity   112
   The Pasta-Making Table   118
   Rustic Chic   124
   For Fun and Games   130
   Old Tobacco Store   138
   Fall Recipes   146

WINTER   166
   Stone Kitchen   168
   The Flavors of Yesteryear   172
   Poor Man's Marble   178
   The Charm of Yesteryear   184
   Gnomes' Kitchen   188
   Winter Recipes   196

INTRODUCTION

A country kitchen has always been a place for empathy.

An old pasta-making table, a well-stocked pantry, a fire burning in the focarile – the kitchen hearth – or a faded tile can awaken a dormant memory; evoking a flavor from childhood, a sunny day, someone dear, a moment of tranquility, or a vacation. It can even convey to you the desire for slowing down the pace of life, for taking time for yourself and loved ones, for allowing yourself the pleasure of choosing the produce from this very earth and mixing them with the only aim of making a meal, of enjoying every preparation step, before abandoning yourself to the flavors.

Each kitchen is a private and intimate place to be shared only with those you love and which is able to reveal itself through recipes.

Suspended in time and space as they are, country kitchens are a cave of delights, a secret world or a magic box where things happen, where some things are transformed and others invented in the midst of a special ritual. Always different. Always enchanting. The ritual varies depending on the people it is for, the atmosphere created, the colors and smells that envelop you, and the emotions involved. In short, it is the mélange of all of these extraordinary elements that gives rural gastronomy the features of the kitchens where its dishes are prepared and served.

This is a book about cooking and country kitchens. It represents the celebration of certain alchemies of flavors, and the very special places where these flavors are born. It shows kitchens of people who have lived in country houses for years, of people who have come back to rediscover them after many years, of those who make occasional use of them, and of those who are suddenly taken by the urge to have one. The book also offers recipes that, like the places where they are prepared, have remained intact since their beginnings, or which have been revisited, recalled, or rewritten.

The cooking and country kitchens exude simplicity or sophistication. They are basic or elaborate. They have been selected on the basis of their appeal, personality, or natural charm, where each object, choice, or action, on the one hand, and combination, and presentation on the other, tells a different story, and has a different meaning and value.

These are, therefore, much loved, studied and though out kitchens and ways of cooking. These kitchens were designed to be a perfect place to play with the gifts each season brings to the garden and vegetable patch, and a place to invite loved ones to share a table and a feast of flavors.

Fiorella Congedo

SPRING

THE GRACE OF TIME

This fascinating old kitchen could be the threshold to another dimension, like a time machine. A vision in sky blue and white. It features antique tiles running the length of the countertop against the back wall, shaped and enameled wood on cabinets for a paneling effect, an old enameled kitchen scale, a traditional country table, a collection of antique rustic ceramics, and an old dish rack. Everything exudes poetry.

The charm continues beyond this space into the splendid patio-garden, where the blue painted wrought iron bistro table and chairs are enveloped by thousands of green hues and the alchemy of aromatic herbs.

First, the old kitchen.

Left, an image of the kitchen from the corner of the table covered in a checked table cloth.

Above, a detail of the old cabinets, with the old pale blue enameled kitchen scale.

Previous pages, old porcelain pieces and the dining room.

On these pages, the dining room seen from the living area, and the outdoor dining area on the terrace.

COUNTRY ARISTOCRAT

This is a country house surrounded by an immense park. The kitchen has been restored to its former glory and is bathed with light in the early hours of the afternoon.

A large glazed door connects the interior with the outdoor eating area, where a monumental stone table stands under a wrought iron gazebo, offering shelter in all seasons. In the middle of the spacious kitchen is an imposing flue decorated with a number of antique pieces salvaged from the collapse of an outbuilding on the property, and with magnificent original tiles, hung in groups of four just like pictures set into the white of the wall.

First, the large stone table under the green gazebo in the garden connected to the kitchen.

Left, exterior view, entrance to the kitchen and detail of the table.

Above, the large sculptured flue with a restored antique carved piece.

NATURE INSIDE

A large L-shaped kitchen/dining area projected onto a beautiful old courtyard. Outdoor paving tiles salvaged from an old country house line the floor of the entire room. The ceiling is white-washed wattle.

The highlight of this space is the large countertop, with a clay surface without protruding edges. It appears to reflect the irregular lines of the rock jutting out of facing wall, which was left intact and reinvented as an additional surface to hold kitchen utensils.

First, the dining area bathed in light with a whitewashed wattle ceiling, an old floor paved in outdoor tiles, and a table with chairs painted in pastel colors.

Double page, the long brick and plaster countertop with projecting rock and polished surfaces so as not to leave any sharp edges.

On these pages, details of the kitchen with old rustic furniture.

AN ARCHITECT'S REFUGE

This large country house, the refuge of an internationally-renowned architect, is characterized by an interesting blend of old and new. Facing twin sideboards, there is an industrial kitchen with an aspect that is softened by the presence of a traditional refectory table. The twin sideboards in the dining room, combining with the large stone fireplace, are Provençal in style, and have been stripped and painted pale blue. They are topped with ceramic pieces crafted into lamps. The old solid wood table is in the center of this space and contrasts with designer chairs.

First, the spacious dining area with a fireplace in the background and the large refectory table surrounded by chairs designed by Philippe Starck for Kartell.

Facing page, a side view o the dining area with two 18th-century sideboards from Emilia-Romagna enameled in blue.

Above, a modern stainless steel industrial kitchen purposefully contrasting with the twin 18th-century sideboards with their antique appearance.

SETTING THE STAGE

The old herbalist's counter was found in the old warehouse of a junk dealer and became the starting point. The rest was built around it. The kitchen of this parish presbytery was designed this way, in order to let this extraordinary piece become the focal point of the stage setting, the absolute protagonist, the star.

The licorice-painted stone kitchen countertop, the white-enameled sink and the wooden cabinet doors came later. Harmonizing with the neutral color scheme, a long upper shelf between two walls exudes discreet grace and balance. On the opposite wall, an alcove is created by a white fireplace flanked by divans using stonework, two of the best seats from which to enjoy the show, the tranquility and flavors of a far off time.

First, the ceramic sink nestling in the gray clay countertop on the other side of the central counter.

On the previous pages, the large herbalist's counter – the real protagonist of this spacious kitchen – also used as a breakfast table.

Side, the inside of the herbalist's counter – used as storage – is covered with a raw linen curtain.

Old jars filled with sweet and savory delicacies line the long clay shelf limiting both sides of the area.

ASPARAGUS CANAPÉS

INGREDIENTS

► *2 eggs*

► *½ lb asparagus tips*

► *extra virgin olive oil*

► *home-made bread*

► *salt*

Boil the eggs. Mash with two tablespoons of oil, salt, and the asparagus tips previously boiled in a little salted water. Spread the cream over toasted slices of home-made bread.

ARTICHOKE QUICHE

INGREDIENTS

- ► *½ lb shortcrust pastry*
- ► *10 artichokes*
- ► *1 onion*
- ► *2 eggs*
- ► *¼ lb parmesan cheese*
- ► *1 ¼ cups velouté sauce*
- ► *extra virgin olive oil*
- ► *salt and pepper to taste*

Clean the artichokes and stems. Cut the artichokes in lengths and the stems into small pieces. Put the oil in a shallow saucepan and brown the finely-chopped onion. Add the artichoke and stems just as the onion is turning golden. Add salt and cook on very low heat with the lid on. Leave to cool a little and blend, before adding the eggs, parmesan, pepper, and thickened velouté sauce Stir all the ingredients together well. Roll out the dough to a thickness of about 1/12 inches and use it to cover a mold that has been previously greased with butter and flour. Spread the artichoke filling over it. Bake at 350°F for about 50 minutes. The quiche should be eaten the same day so that the pastry is easy to cut.

BAKED RING OF RICE WITH VEGETABLES

INGREDIENTS

- ► *½ lb short, round-grained rice*
- ► *⅓ lb king trumpet mushrooms*
- ► *1 eggplant*
- ► *3-4 zucchini*
- ► *⅓ lb green peas*
- ► *5-7 ripe cherry tomatoes*
- ► *½ onion*
- ► *1 garlic clove*
- ► *1 egg*
- ► *⅞ cups of thickened velouté sauce*
- ► *8-10 lettuce leaves*
- ► *¾ oz butter*
- ► *extra virgin olive oil and salt to taste*

Pour ½ cup of oil in a large frying pan. Brown the chopped onion and garlic. When golden, add the mushroom, eggplant, zucchini, diced tomatoes and peas. Cook on high heat, stirring carefully from time to time. Salt to taste. When the vegetables are cooked and the liquid has evaporated, leave to cool a little. Add the velouté sauce, the egg and the al dente (just cooked) boiled rice. Mix well.

Scald the lettuce leaves in boiling salted water. Use butter to grease a ring mold with a lid. Line the base and sides with lettuce leaves. Add the vegetable mixture and bake at 350°F for approximately 30 minutes. Take out of the oven and allow to cool for a few minutes. Remove from the mold to a serving dish for presentation.

RICH SPRING SOUP

INGREDIENTS

▶ 6-7 tablespoons extra virgin olive oil

▶ ½ onion

▶ 1 garlic clove

▶ 5-6 ripe cherry tomatoes

▶ parsley

▶ ½ lb small and tender broad beans

▶ ⅓ lb green peas

▶ 6 artichoke hearts

▶ 2 bunches dandelion greens

▶ 2 pints stock

▶ meatballs

▶ croutons

▶ salt to taste

▶ For the meatballs:

▶ ½ lb minced beef

▶ 1 egg

▶ 7-8 tablespoons breadcrumbs

▶ 3 tablespoons grated parmesan

▶ finely chopped parsley

▶ fine salt (to taste)

Place the oil, sliced onion, garlic, the seeded, peeled, and diced tomatoes, chopped parsley, beans, peas and the artichoke hearts cut into wedges in a saucepan. Fry for ten minutes. Add the chopped dandelion greens. Add the stock, cover and cook on low heat. Prepare the meatballs: mix all of the ingredients together and make small balls. Add to the soup. Serve steaming hot with croutons.

ROAST LAMB

INGREDIENTS

► *2 ½ lb leg of lamb*

► *bay leaf*

► *rosemary*

► *sage*

► *½ cup white wine*

► *2 lbs potatoes*

► *bread crumbs*

► *extra virgin olive oil and salt to taste*

Cut the leg into pieces. Marinade in water, oil, fine salt, rosemary, bay leaf and sage for at least two hours. Place on a sheet pan and pour 2 ladlefuls of the marinade and the wine over it. When half cooked, add the previously sliced potatoes. Sprinkle with bread crumbs. Roast at 350°F until the water has evaporated completely and the potato and lamb is cooked.

PENNYROYAL ARTICHOKES

INGREDIENTS

- ▶ *artichokes*
- ▶ *juice of 1 lemon*
- ▶ *5-6 teaspoons extra virgin olive oil*
- ▶ *½ onion*
- ▶ *1 garlic clove*
- ▶ *2 tablespoons chopped parsley*
- ▶ *1 handful European pennyroyal leaves.*
- ▶ *salt and pepper to taste*

Remove the tougher outer leaves from the artichokes. Cut off the tips of the central cones. Cut into wedges and submerge a little at a time into water mixed with the lemon juice. Clean the stems by removing the outer filaments. Chop and add to the artichoke heart pieces.

Heat the extra virgin olive oil in a frying pan with the garlic. Remove the garlic before it darkens. Add the artichoke and chopped onion. Brown slowly. Season. Add a little water if necessary. When cooked, add the chopped parsley and the pennyroyal leaves. Sprinkle with pepper.

FRIED PUMPKIN FLOWERS

INGREDIENTS

- ► *15 zucchini flowers*
- ► *⅔ cup flour*
- ► *2-3 eggs*
- ► *½ cup beer*
- ► *5 ½ oz fontina cheese*
- ► *2 tablespoons pickled capers*
- ► *extra virgin olive oil and salt to taste*

Remove the stems. Wash the flowers carefully so that they remain whole. Prepare a batter with the flour, eggs, a pinch of salt, and the chilled beer. Beat well until the mixture is uniform and runny.

Fill each flower with 2-3 capers and 2-3 small pieces of fontina. Twist the top closed. Dip into the batter and deep fry in very hot oil. Place over paper towel to drain the excess oil. Serve very hot.

CARAMEL FRUIT SKEWERS

INGREDIENTS

- ▶ *2 peaches*
- ▶ *4 apricots*
- ▶ *8 large strawberries*
- ▶ *2 bananas*
- ▶ *juice of 1 lemon*
- ▶ *7/8 cup sugar*

Halve, pit and cut the peaches and apricots into pieces. Wash together with the strawberries. Peel the bananas. Cut into pieces and pour lemon juice over them to stop discoloration.

Put the sugar in a small saucepan with two tablespoons of water. Leave to melt on a low heat. Stir until it begins to darken and caramelize. Remove from the heat.

On wooden skewers arrange pieces of peach, banana, and apricot, alternating them with pieces of strawberry. Place the skewers on a serving dish. Pour caramel over the fruit and allow to solidify. Serve cold.

MIMOSA CAKE

INGREDIENTS

- ▸ *sponge cake*
- ▸ *Chantilly cream*
- ▸ *1 can pineapple slices*
- ▸ *1 small glass of maraschino liqueur*
- ▸ *1 ¾ cups fresh whipped cream*

For the sponge cake:

- ▸ *4 eggs*
- ▸ *1 cup sugar*
- ▸ *1 ¾ cups flour*
- ▸ *1 packet dry yeast*
- ▸ *¾ oz butter*

For the Chantilly cream:

- ▸ *3 egg yolks*
- ▸ *5 tablespoons flour*
- ▸ *10 tablespoons sugar*
- ▸ *2 cups milk*
- ▸ *rind of 1 lemon*
- ▸ *1 ¼ cups fresh whipped cream*

Prepare the sponge cake and Chantilly cream in the normal way.

Cut the sponge horizontally through the middle and set the top aside. Hollow out the lower half and use your hands to crumble the inner part that has been taken out. Cut up 5-6 of the canned pineapple slices. Mix the liquid from the can with the maraschino liqueur and apply with a brush to the base, the sides and the top of the sponge cake.

Fill the base with alternating layers of cream, pineapple pieces, and cake crumbs. Put the top half back on to close. Spread whipped cream all over the dessert. Sprinkle with the remaining cake that has been very finely crumbled.

ROSE PETAL JELLY

INGREDIENTS

- ▶ *7 oz wild rose petals*
- ▶ *3 ½ cups sugar*
- ▶ *½ cup honey*
- ▶ *water*

Mix the freshly picked wild rose petals with the sugar and honey. Add three tablespoons of water to melt the sugar and cook in a bain-marie until the desired consistency is achieved.

SUMMER

IN BLACK AND WHITE

There is an old range. Beautiful, imposing and shiny. Its white tiles contrast strongly with the black iron doors and the color of brass . The kitchen opens onto a flower-filled porch and is decorated with several collections – objects carefully selected one by one and grouped by families to be admired as statues on an altar, as works of art arranged in rows, or as witnesses, companions, and accomplices to the extraordinary alchemy of aromas and flavors.

First page, a corner of the range with a collection of decorated pitchers on the shelves.

Double page, a general perspective of the kitchen with white wooden cabinets.

On these pages, the picturesque doorway leading from the kitchen to the garden, and the large fireplace with black and white tiles like those on the floor.

THE PERFECT BALANCE

Each piece in this small country kitchen, full of charm and a unique atmosphere, tells a story of its own. The kitchen is the fruit of a passion to evoke childhood memories, of the search for obsolete but amusing things, and of the desire to find a new vocation for them, even the things that may seem the most humble.

First, the outdoor eating area with wrought iron table and chairs under a leafy grapevine.

Double page, panoramic view of the kitchen with the solid wood table in the middle and two symmetrical dressers on either side of a central niche.

Left, the enameled work table used as additional surface space. Above, detail of wicker baskets and old frying pans.

TURQUOISE DELIGHT

The large range has an old-fashioned charm; its doors and drawers faced with iron and brass are still intact. The kitchen also features copper objects hanging on the wall, patterned floor tiles and has an imposing, almost monumental feel to it. And then there is turquoise: bright, cheery and light. In bursts, it dominates the scene. The playfulness of turquoise chairs around a table of dark wood breaks the austerity of the stonework. Turquoise colors a large old cabinet used as a pantry. It is as if this kitchen had two souls. As if, one the one hand, it suffers the weight of the passing years, while, on the other, it puts on a brave face with a large dose of irony.

Turquoise is featured, clearly dominating the shades of black and copper, and over the white tiles.

Double page, a sweeping view of the kitchen, with the L-shaped countertop to the left and the large fireplace to the right.

Page on the left, the small glass cabinet showing shelves decorated with scallop-edged cloth.

Above, view of the kitchen with the large blue closet in the background.

AQUAMARINE HUMOR

Aquamarine. A house, a kitchen, a color. This small aristocratic country house gives off its own special vibrations and charm – its own humor. It is a reflection that is intensified as it passes through the glazed wall and out to the small vegetable garden behind the house. This reflection is toned down in the dining room where the sideboard is located. With its color, it has determined the basic design scheme of the living areas. The same reflection is patent in an intermittent fashion in the checked floor, which is decorated with old tiles. It is a reflection with an embroidery-like presence that is at once both simple and valuable, and which decorates the kitchen countertop from one end to the other.

Previous page, a view of the dining area with the large living space in the background.

Left page, the large kitchen fireplace and a detail of the checked floor.

Above, the countertop lined with cement floor tiles and the contrast between the rising, step-like shelves and downward lines of the countertop curtains.

On the previous pages, the passage connecting the kitchen with the dining area. The pale blue sideboard has been placed in a recess left by the vault.

Left, the view out to the small garden through a large glazed door.

Above, the dining area with chairs upholstered in old fabrics.

SOPHISTICATED NATURE

This sophisticated country kitchen oozes Provençal charm as it plays with different tones of grey, white and pale blue. These colors are reflected in the cement floor, in the enamel of the chairs, in the *décapé* effect on the closets built into the living stone walls, and in the natural wood of the table. These hues are in turn brought to life by the bright colors of the produce from the fields. This is patent in bunches of *di penda* tomatoes and prickly pear leaf pads hanging from the ceiling to form patterns like garlands from an extraordinary pagan feast in celebration of nature and her portent.

First, a detail of the dining area with a wonderful table sanded back to reveal the natural wood, surrounded by chairs enameled in powder gray.

Double page, the dining area with *di penda* tomatoes and prickly pear leaf pads hanging as if they were part of an art installation.

Left, the grapevine spreads profusely, hiding the small antique cages hanging next to the entrance.

Above, almonds left to dry in the sun.

EGGPLANT MEATBALLS

INGREDIENTS

- ▶ 4 medium eggplants
- ▶ 1 garlic clove
- ▶ 2 eggs
- ▶ 1 cup coarse bread crumbs
- ▶ 2 oz grated pecorino cheese
- ▶ 1 ⅛ cups grated parmesan
- ▶ 1 sprig of parsley
- ▶ 3-4 tablespoons pickled capers
- ▶ salt and pepper to taste
- ▶ very fine bread crumbs
- ▶ oil for frying

Without removing the skin, cut the eggplant into large pieces. Boil in salted water. Drain well, pressing with your hands. Chop coarsely and mash in a bowl with a fork. Add the whole eggs, the coarse bread crumbs, all of the grated cheese, the chopped parsley, garlic, and freshly ground pepper. Mash together. Ensure all of the ingredients are well mixed. Make elongated meatballs. Roll in the fine bread crumbs and deep fry in very hot oil. Serve hot or at room temperature.

Pizza with rocket salad and cherry tomato

Ingredients

- *2 cups flour*
- *¼ oz packet brewer's yeast*
- *2 tablespoons lukewarm water*
- *1 teaspoon salt*
- *½ cup water*
- *1 lb diced mozzarella*
- *10-15 cherry tomatoes*
- *abundant arugula*
- *extra virgin olive oil and salt to taste*

First, prepare dough for the base by dissolving the brewer's yeast in the lukewarm water. Add 2 tablespoons flour. Place the dough in a floured bowl. Cover and leave to rise in a warm place until the dough has doubled in size.

Prepare more dough by placing a little flour and salt on a kneading board and adding lukewarm water. Knead until the dough is not too hard. Combine the two batches of dough and knead energetically for a good while.

Once the dough has doubled in size, and pressing with your finger leaves a small imprint, divide into four pieces and shape each into a circle. Place on a sheet pan greased with oil. Cover each pizza with the chopped tomatoes, abundant mozzarella and drizzle oil over them. Bake in a preheated oven at 425°F for 20 minutes. Remove from the oven. Cover with fresh chopped arugula. Serve immediately.

PASTA ALLA CRUDAIOLA

INGREDIENTS

- ► *1 lb pasta (orecchiette, ditaloni or spaghetti)*
- ► *10 oz firm ripe cherry tomatoes*
- ► *½ lb cacioricotta cheese*
- ► *1 teaspoon oregano*
- ► *20-30 basil leaves*
- ► *peperoncino chili*
- ► *extra virgin olive oil and salt to taste*

Chop the tomatoes into very small pieces. Place in a dish that can be used for serving the pasta. Add the oregano, finely chopped basil, peperoncino, grated cacioricotta and abundant oil. Cook the pasta in salted water. Strain and mix in the bowl with the ready-prepared condiment.

BROAD BEANS AND CHICORY

INGREDIENTS

- ▶ 1 lb broad beans
- ▶ 1 garlic clove
- ▶ 2 bay leaves
- ▶ ½ onion
- ▶ 3-4 cherry tomatoes
- ▶ 1 sprig of parsley
- ▶ 1 potato
- ▶ 2 lbs wild chicory greens
- ▶ extra virgin olive oil and salt to taste

Soak the broad beans overnight before removing the skin. Simmer in an uncovered earthenware saucepan in salted water with the clove of garlic, bay leaves, onion, tomatoes, parsley, and the peeled whole potato. When cooked, process with a food mill to make a purée.

Wash the chicory greens several times and boil in salted water. Accompany the puréed beans with the chicory. Drizzle with plentiful olive oil before serving.

MEATLOAF WITH BASIL

INGREDIENTS

- ½ lb veal
- ½ lb chicken breast meat
- ¼ lb ham
- ¼ cup grated parmesan cheese
- 2 eggs
- 1 cup fresh bread crumbs (using sliced bread)
- a little milk
- 20 fresh basil leaves
- nutmeg
- dry bread crumbs
- oil for greasing
- salt and pepper to taste

Mince the meat. Mix all of the ingredients together with your hands and make a thick and very compact sausage. Lightly coat with dry bread crumbs. Use a brush to grease a sheet of aluminum foil with oil. Place the meatloaf in the center. Wrap with the foil without pressing and close well. Turn the oven to 350°F and bake for 40 minutes, turning the meatloaf over after 30 minutes. Remove from the oven. Leave to cool in the foil before unwrapping and cutting into slices.

Serve hot with ratatouille or sautéed peas, or cold with mayonnaise or tomato vinaigrette, made by blending the pulp of 2 or 3 ripe tomatoes with three tablespoons of oil, the juice of half a lemon, salt, and pepper.

BITTERSWEET EGGPLANT

INGREDIENTS

- ► *4 eggplants*
- ► *2 tablespoons sugar*
- ► *1 cup vinegar*
- ► *extra virgin olive oil and salt to taste*

Cut the eggplant into pieces. Deep fry a few at a time. Salt. Combine the sugar and vinegar in a frying pan. When the sugar dissolves, add the eggplant. Stir constantly while heating so that it absorbs the flavor. Serve at room temperature.

MINT OMELET

INGREDIENTS

- ▶ *5 ½ oz ricotta cheese*
- ▶ *5 eggs*
- ▶ *¼ cup grated parmesan cheese*
- ▶ *mint*
- ▶ *extra virgin olive oil*

Beat the eggs with the ricotta and grated parmesan. Add a handful of mint leaves. Pour into a frying pan containing two tablespoons of very hot olive oil. Cook the omelet on both sides. Place over paper towel to drain the excess oil. Serve hot.

LEMON BLACKBERRIES

INGREDIENTS

▶ *1 cup blackberries*

▶ *2 tablespoons sugar*

▶ *lemon*

Cover the blackberries with the sugar in a bowl and refrigerate. Drizzle with lemon juice or lemon liqueur when serving.

FIG AND GRAPE CROSTATA (TART)

INGREDIENTS

For the shortcrust pastry:

- 2 cups flour
- 4 tablespoons sugar
- 3 ½ oz butter
- 1 egg
- a pinch of fine salt
- milk
- 4-5 dry cookies

For the pastry cream:

- 2 cups milk
- 3 egg yolks
- ⅝ cup sugar
- 5 tablespoons potato starch
- 1 packet vanillin

For the topping:

- 3-4 figs
- 1 bunch black grapes
- 1 bunch white grapes
- ½ cup fruit gelatin

Prepare the pastry by mixing together the flour, sugar, butter (previously melted in a bain-marie), egg, salt, and as much milk as can be absorbed in order to obtain homogeneous dough. Stand in the refrigerator for 30 minutes. Roll out the dough and use it to cover the base and sides of a mold previously greased with butter and flour. Bake at 390°F until the surface turns a light golden color.

Make up a pastry cream in the usual way and pour it into the tart after lining the base with crushed cookie crumbs.

Cut up the figs and place them over the cream together with the grapes. Cover the surface with fruit gelatin diluted with a tablespoon of very hot water. Serve.

PRICKLY PEAR JELLY

INGREDIENTS

▶ *9 lbs prickly pear*

▶ *8 ¾ cups sugar*

▶ *1 lemon*

Put the cleaned prickly pear in a stew pot with sugar and the grated rind of one lemon. After standing for two hours, boil for 15 minutes. Crush through a sieve to remove the seeds. Return to the pot and cook. It is ready when a spoonful of the mixture does not spread when placed on a plate. Store in preheated, hermetically-sealed jars until they cool completely.

AUTUMN

THE ELEGANCE OF SIMPLICITY

This small, old-style kitchen has a layout based on alternating filled spaces with voids. A solid wood table stands in the center of the room, surrounded by chairs with rush seats and covered with a plastic tablecloth to protect the top from stains. Above it hangs a light made from a tamis sieve.

Two arches in the far wall frame service areas in two symmetrical recesses. On the right, a pantry is enclosed by an old-style curtain, while on the right, a stainless-steel countertop runs the length of the wall bordered by two rows of antique tiles with geometric patterns. The old alcoves in the room have been preserved and reutilized as auxiliary surfaces and valuable storage spaces.

First, a detail of the kitchen, where each alcove is made use of as a storage space.

On the previous pages, three details on the left, and a view of the kitchen on the right.

On these pages, two large alcoves, the first used to install the kitchen countertop, and the second used as a pantry enclosed by a curtain.

THE PASTA-MAKING TABLE

This small kitchen in an outbuilding belonging to a country house features antique majolica tiles joined in a panel and surrounded by white tiles to make the colors stand out even more.

Attention is also drawn to the striped curtains covering the shelves under the long countertop. The real focal point of the setting stands in the middle of the room. It is a magnificent work table previously used to make pasta, as evidenced by the rolling pin and kneading board, which are still kept in one side and removed as needed. These are genuine articles that have been marked by the passing of time and given shape by years of use.

First, the kitchen table covered with a white tablecloth with crocheted inserts. The living area is in the background.

Previous pages, on the left, the pretty kitchen table with a marble top, antique glass drawer pull, and on the side, the removable rolling pin and kneading board for use in preparing home-made pasta. On the right, a corner of the kitchen with fuchsia and white canvas.

On these pages, a detail of the brick and tile countertop with the central collage of differing antique majolica tiles in blues laid out like a tapestry.

RUSTIC CHIC

This is a kitchen adapted to the space of a small country house and divided into two areas. The range and countertops were built into one of the recesses in the old structure in a process that follows the line of the old stonework. The sink is located in a transit area. It is out of immediate view and can be hidden behind customized wooden panels. The old wall recesses have been restored and are open to view throughout the space. Period ceramic pieces and silverware are displayed in them. Home appliances and a large refrigerator are confined to a service area to the rear of the house.

First, entrance to the kitchen, divided into two well-camouflaged areas.

Left, an image offering a glimpse of the dining area.

Above, the two kitchen spaces: the cooking area in the recess and the washing area.

The dining area looking toward the living area.

A recess in the kitchen featuring a shelf.

FOR FUN AND GAMES

An old rural building, once used as a shelter for animals and to store the harvest, has been transformed into a fascinating country residence, where white is used as a color instead of a non-color.

The kitchen, with a form and layout not unlike that of a loft, is located at the far right side of the space. Slightly hidden behind a low partition wall and blurred by trick of perspective, it appears almost by surprise. Using an old stone laundry wash basin as a sink is an original idea, as is the use of early 20th-century paving tiles to line the walls on both sides of the windows. There are two rectangular, solid wood tables in the middle of the dwelling. They are placed one against the other to form an almost perfect square and are accompanied by brightly colored chairs.

To complete the picture, there is an Indian tapestry hanging on the back wall. An old kitchen dresser, restored with milky white enamel, runs along the right wall, while an elegant chandelier hangs from the ceiling.

On the previous pages, close up of the old laundry wash basin used as a sink, an old tin bucket, the container for oil, and a set of market scales. The large kitchen dresser finished in butter-colored enamel.

Double page, general view of the old, almost identical solid wood tables placed one against the other to create a square, and brightly painted chairs with rush seats. The chandelier and oriental tapestry on the back wall mark a clear contrast.

Left, a view of the dining area with its solid Indian table and large fireplace.

Above, a perspective of the living area as seen from the kitchen.

OLD TOBACCO STORE

An old barn used to store tobacco has been given new life, although the soul of the building has been profoundly respected. The kitchen is basic and humble – its simplicity has pared all of its functions to a bare minimum – and here the beating heart of the house is once again the kitchen hearth, as it was in old times. The subtle technique of bringing objects and colors, fabrics and nuances, atmospheres and lights into play creates a unique feel, which is discovered from different angles and perspectives. It is a place where a basket of apples, a garlic bulb, and a prickly pear leaf pad are transformed into decoration, grace, and poetry.

First page, a view of the old remodeled tobacco barn.

Previous pages, the extreme simplicity of the countertop and the exposed stone wall. Below, a corner of the living area. Right, an old restored table used to hold a small collection of iron containers.

Double page, a general view of the living area looking toward the front door. On the table in the middle of the room is a nativity scene made from old papier mâché figures.

Left, detail of the living area. Above, the pale blue dish rack with antique ceramic pieces.

HERB CHEESE BOATS

INGREDIENTS

For the boats:

- ► *5 ½ oz shortcrust pastry*
- ► *dab of butter*
- ► *handful of flour*

For the filling:

- ► *5 ½ oz soft cheese*
- ► *finely chopped chives, basil and parley*
- ► *2-3 sun-dried tomatoes*

Line small butter and flour-greased oval-shaped molds with shortcrust pastry. Bake at 350°F. Remove from the molds. Fill the boats with a mixture made from the cheese and the chives, basil, and parsley. Sprinkle with the finely chopped sun-dried tomatoes.

Vegetable foccacia

Ingredients

- ▶ 12 ½ cups flour
- ▶ 1 cube of yeast dissolved in a little warm milk
- ▶ 1 demitasse (2.5 oz) oil
- ▶ 1 whole egg
- ▶ milk for kneading
- ▶ extra virgin olive oil and salt to taste

For the filling:

- ▶ 2 ¼ lbs boiled and chopped curly endive
- ▶ 2 coarsely chopped scallions
- ▶ stoned black olives
- ▶ chopped peperoncino chili
- ▶ ½ lb peeled tomatoes

Make a mound with the flour on a kneading board and form a well in the center. Pour in the milk with the dissolved yeast together with the oil, a pinch of salt, and the egg. Knead. Add milk from time to time until you obtain a dough that is not too soft, but smooth and springy. Set aside to rise.

Prepare the filling: pour a little oil in a frying pan, add the scallion and brown. Drain the endive and add, together with the tomato in slices and sauté for about 10-15 minutes. Finally add the chili and black olives and stir.

Grease a heat-resistant dish with oil and flour and form a layer of dough. Cover with the filling. Place another layer of dough over it. Brush oil over the dough and bake in a preheated oven at 390°F for 45-50 minutes until the surface of the foccacia turns a golden color. Serve hot or at room temperature.

FUSILLI IN PUMPKIN CREAM

INGREDIENTS

- ► 12 ½ oz fusilli *(pasta twists)* or farfalle *(bow-tie pasta)*
- ► *1 lb pumpkin pulp*
- ► *5 medium scallions, finely sliced*
- ► *stock to taste*
- ► *½ lb soft cheese*
- ► *extra virgin olive oil and salt to taste*
- ► *1 ⅛ cups grated parmesan*

Pour a half cup of oil into a saucepan and add the sliced scallions. When browned, add the chopped pumpkin and sauté. Then simmer until it becomes mushy, adding a ladleful of stock from time to time.

Process the pumpkin and soft cheese in a blender. Cook the pasta until it is al dente. Strain and place in a pasta serving dish. Mix well with the pumpkin sauce and the parmesan. Serve the pasta steaming hot.

PASTA E FAGIOLI *(PASTA AND WHITE BEAN SOUP)*

INGREDIENTS

- ▶ *½ lb dried haricot beans*
- ▶ *14 oz tubetti pasta (macaroni)*
- ▶ *1 finely chopped celery stalk*
- ▶ *½ medium onion, sliced*
- ▶ *5 peeled tomatoes*
- ▶ *1 garlic clove*
- ▶ *3 oz pancetta*
- ▶ *½ cup extra virgin olive oil*
- ▶ *salt and pepper to taste*

Soak the beans overnight with a little coarse salt. Cook in an earthenware saucepan. Purée two ladlefuls of the beans. Pour the oil in a saucepan. Brown the onion and garlic. Add the celery, chopped tomatoes and the diced pancetta. Add the beans. Let it boil for a few minutes to soak in the flavor. Add the pasta, cooked al dente *and the puréed beans. Stir. Stand for two minutes and serve with plenty of freshly-ground black pepper.*

CUTLETS WITH GARLIC AND BAY LEAF CROSTINI

INGREDIENTS

For the cutlets:

- ► *1 lb minced pork*
- ► *2 eggs*
- ► *¼ cup rosé*
- ► *½ cup extra virgin olive oil*
- ► *1 sprig of parsley*
- ► *1 garlic clove*
- ► *5 tablespoons grated pecorino cheese*
- ► *day-old white bread without crust with quantity equal to half the volume of the meat*
- ► *salt to taste*

- ► *white bread slices*
- ► *milk*
- ► *bay leaves*
- ► *extra virgin olive oil to taste*

For the cutlets: mash together the ingredients ensuring they are well mixed. Make 3-inch long oval cutlets.

Cut the white bread into slices the same size as the cutlets. Soak in the milk with a pinch of salt. Make up skewers a little shorter than the sheet pan alternating a slice of bread with a cutlet, and placing a bay leaf between both. Bake at 350°F for 20-30 minutes. While cooking, brush the leftover milk and a little oil over the cutlets to stop them from drying out.

MUSHROOMS AU GRATIN

INGREDIENTS

▶ *1 lb wild mushrooms*

▶ *1 garlic clove, finely chopped*

▶ *chopped parsley*

▶ *4 tablespoons dry bread crumbs*

▶ *3 tablespoons grated cheese*

▶ *extra virgin olive oil, salt and pepper*

Arrange the cleaned mushrooms close together – almost overlapping – in a baking dish. Mix the other ingredients together and cover the mushrooms. Drizzle a little olive oil. Bake at 350°F for about 30 minutes.

FRIED MINI-PIZZAS

INGREDIENTS

For the base:

- ► *3 ¾ cups flour*
- ► *½ oz (2 packets) brewer's yeast*
- ► *a pinch of salt*

For the filling:

- ► *½ lb peeled tomatoes in pieces*
- ► *1 tablespoon sugar*
- ► *1 garlic clove*
- ► *10 ½ oz mozzarella cheese for pizzas*
- ► *oregano*
- ► *chopped basil*
- ► *extra virgin olive oil and salt to taste*

Place the flour, the yeast dissolved in lukewarm water, and the salt on a kneading board. Make dough for a pizza base and stand for two hours. Flatten the dough to a 2/3" thickness. Cut out rectangles measuring 2" x 2/3". Lay over a dish towel and leave to rise another 30 minutes. Deep fry. Take out and drain the excess oil over paper towel.

Prepare the filling: brown the garlic in a little oil. Add the drained tomato pieces. After 10 minutes, add the sugar, salt, oregano and basil. Cook the sauce until it becomes very thick. When the mini pizzas are just warm, cut three sides open with kitchen scissors and fill with the sauce and a few pieces of mozzarella.

Place one by one on a sheet pan. Before serving, place in a hot oven that has been turned off to melt the mozzarella.

PERFUMED QUINCE

INGREDIENTS

▶ *10 medium ripe quinces*

▶ *sugar*

▶ *cinnamon*

Wash the quinces. Place on a sheet pan and bake. Peel the still-hot quinces. Cut in wedges. Arrange them one by one on a serving dish. Sprinkle with sugar and powdered cinnamon. Allow them to stand and absorb the flavor for 10-12 hours before serving.

MONT BLANC AUX MARRONS

INGREDIENTS

- ► *2 ¼ lbs cleaned chestnuts*
- ► *⅞ cup confectioner's sugar*
- ► *2 pints milk*
- ► *1 vanilla bean*
- ► *2 cups fresh whipped cream*
- ► *meringues*
- ► *marrons glacés*

Cleaning the chestnuts: rinse the chestnuts quickly in cold water and make a cut on the rounded part of the husk; the cut must penetrate the husk to reach the inner skin. Place the chestnuts in a saucepan and cover with water. Boil for 10 minutes until part of the husk opens. Peel them while still hot, also removing the inner skin covering the nut.

Put the chestnuts in a saucepan. Cook with the milk, confectioner's sugar and vanilla bean until it becomes a purée that comes away from the saucepan. Process the purée in a food mill. Allow it to fall directly into a serving dish so that it forms a mound. Cover with whipped cream and decorate with meringues and marrons glacés.

The whipped cream can be introduced into a pastry bag with a star nozzle and used to decorate only the tip of the dessert, to produce the effect of a snow-capped peak.

GRAPE JELLY

INGREDIENTS

▸ 4 ½ lbs grapes

▸ 1 lb sugar

Separate the individual grapes and wash well. Remove the seeds and place the grapes into a very wide frying pan with the sugar. Place the mixture on high heat until it boils, then lower the heat. Stir from time to time with a wooden spoon until the jelly is dry and at the desired consistency.

WINTER

STONE KITCHEN

The kitchen of this small stone house was reduced to a single corner between two interstices opening out to the garden, and was created with incredible grace, harmony, and taste. Outstanding features include an a sink made from an old earthenware pot, appliances built into housings made of tuff stone and hidden behind old closet doors which have had their central panels removed and replaced with chicken wire, and an old, intact work table in the middle of the dining area bearing all the signs of its age.

Previous page, the small kitchen has been reduced to a corner.

Left, panoramic view of the kitchen, with the sink made from an old glazed earthenware pot and built-in closets with salvaged and remodeled doors. Details of the garden from the kitchen.

Above, the dining area with an old work table in the middle.

THE FLAVORS OF YESTERYEAR

The large range seems stolen from another age – a vision in blue and white – with a fire always burning in the hearth and the old cook book always at hand. This is a place where abundant meals continue to be prepared for so many guests, depending on the season, and following the order of the vegetable garden, the fields and the harvest. Provisions for the coming months are prepared here, in the form of pickles, conserves, cookies, and liqueurs for keeping in enormous pantries. Whole days, even months and years are needed to do things as they were done in olden days. And sometimes, things turn out even better.

First, the image of embers and a line of spice jars.

Double page, a panoramic view of the large range with hand-painted blue and white tiles.

Left, bunches of oregano hang to dry in a corner.

Above, a set of pans and an old kitchen scale.

POOR MAN'S MARBLE

This is a country kitchen that has recently been restored and completely faced with clay, a lime render containing crushed terracotta – known as poor man's marble. The color of earth and sand, it has thousands of subtly changing hues depending on the light, the thickness of the coating, and the angle from which it is seen. To form a contrast, starched white curtains have been hung from wrought iron rods to cover the shelves below the agglomerate countertop. In the middle of the room there is a large table of dark wood surrounded by white-enameled chairs, in a play on the two-tone, L-shaped countertop. There is a small table near the window that has been left in its natural wood tone, simply finished with wax.

First, the large agglomerate countertop stands out from the earth-colored cocciopesto background.

On these pages, two details of the built-in range.

Left, an image of the dining table with the garden visible in the background.

Above, an old solid wood table used as additional surface space.

THE CHARM OF YESTERYEAR

The range appears exactly the same as its original version as found in country houses at the turn of the 20th-century. This kitchen is the result of an intense, almost obsessive search for original tiles in flea markets and antique shops, combined with the meticulous modification of new tiles to achieve a perfect fusion, where it is almost impossible to tell the original from the new.

The old kitchen scale still works. The copper parts and the special light that enhances the gilt objects provide the rest of the magic, taking this kitchen to another dimension in time.

First, the large antique range with its original tiles. Where tiles were missing, others were added with an appearance that reproduced the wear and opacity of time.

Left, a corner of the room with the kitchen hearth still in use.

Above, the old scale.

GNOMES' KITCHEN

This is a country kitchen featuring a sink carved out of stone and old tiles showing signs of years gone by. Everywhere there are stores, provisions, pickles, and bottles. They are stacked over every available surface and arranged according to the date of the seasons. It is as if invisible gnomes had hidden their secret treasures here, among the lace curtains, pots and pans hanging from the ceiling, and strangely-shaped and extravagant objects.

First, the store room next to the kitchen.

On the previous pages, corners of the kitchen filled with food, packets, objects of use, and others that are no longer in use, which have found their place and meaning within the whole setting over time. Romantic and retro, the door with a ceramic knob and embroidered curtain.

Double page, a perspective that is so beautiful and full of life that it looks like a painting.

On these pages, the outside dining area covered by a matted cane canopy with an old bench a little out of sight.

VEGETABLE MEATBALLS

INGREDIENTS

- ▶ *10½ oz wild chicory greens*
- ▶ *1 lb boiled potatoes*
- ▶ *garlic*
- ▶ *parsley*
- ▶ *thyme*
- ▶ *marjoram*
- ▶ *8 oz pecorino cheese*
- ▶ *dry bread crumbs*
- ▶ *3 eggs*
- ▶ *extra virgin olive oil*
- ▶ *salt and pepper*

Wash the greens several times. Boil in salted water. Strain and beat with the eggs, the finely-chopped herbs, a small amount of garlic, salt and a little pepper. Add the mixture to the potatoes. Add the grated cheese and bread crumbs and mash until the right consistency is obtained. Shape into meatballs. Deep fry in boiling oil. Serve very hot.

WHITE ROSEMARY FOCCACIA

INGREDIENTS

- ► rosemary
- ► 3 ⅔ cups flour
- ► ½ oz (2 packets) yeast
- ► sugar
- ► salt

Knead the flower with lukewarm water, salt, a pinch of sugar, and yeast. Set aside to rise. Line a sheet pan with a ½" layer of dough. Condiment with rosemary and coarse salt. Bake at 425°F for 20 minutes.

SPAGHETTI WITH OREGANO

INGREDIENTS

- ▶ *1 lb spaghetti*
- ▶ *2 lbs firm ripe cherry tomatoes*
- ▶ *2 garlic cloves*
- ▶ *oregano*
- ▶ *parsley*
- ▶ *20 stoned green olives*
- ▶ *extra virgin olive oil and salt to taste*

Wash the tomatoes and cut in halves. Brown two garlic cloves in a saucepan and add the tomato. Salt. Crush with a fork and leave to cook with the lid on for approximately 15 minutes until the tomato pieces have lost their shape and have released their juice. Turn off the heat, add a little oregano, a handful of chopped parsley, and the olives. Cook the spaghetti until it is al dente. Place in a serving dish. Mix with the tomato. Serve as you like – hot or at room temperature.

LASAGNOTTE *(LASAGNE RIBBONS)*
WITH CHICKPEAS

INGREDIENTS

- ▶ *1 lb* lasagnotte *pasta*
- ▶ *¼ lb diced pancetta*
- ▶ *5 ¼ oz chickpeas*

For the chickpeas:

- ▶ *½ carrot*
- ▶ *½ onion*
- ▶ *1 celery stalk*
- ▶ *3-4 tomatoes*
- ▶ *1 sprig of parsley*
- ▶ *1 garlic clove*
- ▶ *finely chopped peperoncino chili*
- ▶ *extra virgin olive oil and salt to taste*

Soak the chickpeas overnight with a little baking soda. Cook with the carrot, onion, celery and tomatoes. When cooked, strain and set aside the stock.

Heat 5-6 tablespoons of extra virgin olive oil in a shallow saucepan with the garlic. Remove the garlic. Brown the pancetta. Add the chickpeas and sauté.

Cut the lasagnotte in four parts. Boil in abundant salted water, stirring frequently. After 8 minutes, strain when almost al dente. Sauté in the saucepan with the pancetta and chickpeas, gradually adding the stock from cooking the chickpeas and carrots until it has been absorbed or evaporated. Serve in a dish with the parsley and peperoncino to taste.

PORK LOIN IN BARRIQUE WINE VINEGAR

INGREDIENTS

► *1 ¾ lbs pork loin*

► *chives*

► *½ cup barrique wine vinegar*

► *1 garlic clove*

► *6-7 pink peppercorns*

► *2-3 sage or bay leaves*

► *2 teaspoons cornstarch*

► *extra virgin olive oil and salt to taste*

Cut the pork into 2" thick pieces. Tie each piece with a chive leaf, winding it around two or three times. Pour cup of oil in a large shallow saucepan. Carefully arrange the pieces in the pan and brown. Add the vinegar and cook for 5 minutes on high heat. Add the garlic, pink peppercorns, sage leaves and a ladleful of hot water. Salt to taste. Cover and cook for 30 minutes. Set the meat aside and keep hot. Remove the garlic and sage and thicken the sauce by gradually adding the cornstarch while stirring constantly. Arrange the pork on a plate for serving. Cover lightly with part of the sauce and pour the leftover into a sauce boat.

Serve the pork very hot accompanied with yellow carrot sticks cooked in butter and glazed scallions.

PEPERONCINO CABBAGE

INGREDIENTS

- ► *½ cabbage*
- ► *peperoncino chili*
- ► *extra virgin olive oil and salt to taste*

Clean the cabbage by removing the largest leaves. Cut into ½" thick strips. Wash, drain, and boil. Pour ½ cup of oil into a large frying pan and add the cabbage when hot. Cook for about 30 minutes, stirring constantly. Add salt and the ground peperoncino.

GARDEN FRITTERS

INGREDIENTS

- ▶ 3 ¼ cups flour
- ▶ ³/₈ oz (1 ½ packets) brewer's yeast
- ▶ ¼ lb zucchini
- ▶ ⅓ lb potatoes
- ▶ 1 onion
- ▶ ⅓ lb ripe and fleshy tomatoes
- ▶ 2 tablespoons pickled capers
- ▶ 4 tablespoons stoned black olives
- ▶ extra virgin olive oil, and salt and pepper to taste

Chop the zucchini, potatoes, onion, and tomatoes. Place in a bowl. Season with a little fine salt and leave to marinade 5-6 hours. Add the capers, chopped olives, and sprinkle a little pepper. Dust with the flour. Stir until the mixture is uniform. Add the yeast dissolved in a little lukewarm water. The mixture has to be very soft.

Deep fry tablespoonfuls of the mixture. Fry several fritters at a time. Place over paper towel to drain the excess oil. Serve very hot.

STUFFED BAKED APPLES

INGREDIENTS

- ► *4 large apples (reinette apples if possible)*
- ► *2 teaspoons orange marmalade*
- ► *6 crumbled* amaretti cookies
- ► *1 ½ oz butter*
- ► *¼ cup sugar*

Wash the apples. Dry and remove the core with a suitable instrument or a sharp knife. Do not peel. Leave the base of the apple intact. Mix the marmalade with the amaretti *and fill the apples. Arrange in a heat-resistant dish. Dab butter on each apple, sprinkle with sugar, and bake at 425°F for approximately 40 minutes.*

ALMOND COOKIES

INGREDIENTS

- ► *9 cups flour*
- ► *3 tablespoons powdered baking ammonia*
- ► *1 ½ ground almonds*
- ► *1 cup sugar*
- ► *½ lb lard*
- ► *5 eggs*
- ► *½ cup milk*
- ► *1 packet ground vanilla bean*

Place the flour, the peeled and ground almonds, sugar, baking ammonia, lard, eggs and vanilla on a kneading board. Knead until all of the ingredients are well mixed. Soften with the milk.

Roll out the dough to a thickness of ½". Cut rectangles measuring 5" x 1 ½". Brush with beaten egg and sprinkle with sugar. Place on a sheet pan greased with butter, leaving space between them. During baking, the cookies expand and could stick to each other. Bake at 350°F until they are golden and crunchy.

ORANGE MARMALADE

INGREDIENTS

▶ *4 ½ lbs very fresh oranges*

▶ *1 lemon*

▶ *sugar*

Wash the fruit well. Peel and cut into quarters. After removing the pith, cut the rinds into fine strips.

Leave to soak for 12 hours in 4 ½ pints of water. Place the mixture in a saucepan and boil until the oranges are reduced to a mush and the rinds are cooked. Weigh them and add their weight in sugar. Return to the heat and boil for a half-hour until it acquires the desired density. Place in hot sterilized jars. Seal and leave upside down to cool.